Dictionary skills
Contents

Teachers' notes	1
Alphabetical order	
Countries	5
Capital cities	6
Class register	7
Advertisers	8
Understanding abbreviations	
Abbreviations	9
Acronyms	10
Dictionary conventions	11
Counties	12
Addresses	13
Using a dictionary to check definitions	
Homophones – 1	14
Homophones – 2	15
Homonyms – 1	16
Homonyms – 2	17
Using a dictionary to encourage scanning	
Close clues – 1	18
Close clues – 2	19
Close clues – 3	20
Using a dictionary to check meaning	
The frog prince	21
The fox	22
The grey squirrel	23
The badger	24
The rabbit	25
Using a thesaurus to extend vocabulary	
Adjectives – 1	26
Adjectives – 2	27
Find another word	28
Using a thesaurus for alternative words	
Replacing 'nice'	29
Replacing 'said'	30
Replacing 'very'	31
Replacing various words	32

Teachers' notes

Introduction
This book consists of a set of photocopiable sheets to be used as a resource for reinforcing and extending dictionary and thesaurus skills for children working at Key Stage 2.

The activities aim to support the implementation of the spelling part of Writing in the National Curriculum for English. They are not designed as teaching tools in themselves, but rather they offer the children opportunities to explore a dictionary and thesaurus. In order to gain the maximum benefit from these pages it is essential that they are incorporated into a learning environment which offers time for talking, listening, thinking, reading and writing.

There is always a danger with photocopiable sheets that children will see them simply as time-fillers and do not use the skills they have practised when they meet them in other situations.

Dictionary skills are a basic literacy requirement for everyone in today's world, throughout their lives. These skills are part of functional reading, enabling children to extend their knowledge through their ability to research and read for information. Using dictionaries is also a way to extend and refine children's use of language. Too often children stay within the familiar vocabulary that they are able both to spell and use. The vocabulary extension activities included in this book will encourage children to become more adventurous and gain excitement from a more explicit use of words.

Aims of this book
- To help children to become familiar with the conventions of a dictionary and a thesaurus.
- To help consolidate the children's knowledge of alphabetical order.
- To draw attention to the careful and appropriate use of words.
- To extend children's vocabulary by using a thesaurus.
- To offer purposeful activities that allow for the differentiation of ability by outcome as well as by task.

Suggestions for helping children to read the dictionary
Many children try to read a dictionary in the same way that they would read a book. They fail to take notice of the punctuation and this distorts the understanding that is one of the main reasons for consulting a dictionary. The teacher needs to

demonstrate how to read the dictionary, explaining how to pause and reflect upon the definition. Some children never really understand why some words are followed by variations of the word while other words only receive one word of explanation. For example (in *The Oxford Children's Dictionary*), the entry 'enlist' is followed by '(enlists, enlisting, enlisted) To join one of the armed services'. Where as 'enmity' is followed by the single entry 'hatred'.

As dictionaries become more complex children often do not understand the critical apparatus that is provided, for example, the pronunciation guides or the abbreviations for the different parts of speech.

Notes on individual activities

Pages 5–8: Alphabetical order

Children have to recognise the value of knowing alphabetical order. They need as many opportunities as possible for using it. The children could help to sort out library tickets or cards, depending on how the school organises its borrowing system. They should take turns to tidy books into alphabetical order according to author, both in the library and in the classroom. Alphabetical order needs to be so well known that the child hardly hesitates when given a task requiring this knowledge. The first of these activities is concerned with second letter alphabetical order and then they progress to second/third letter.

Extension activities

The children could be encouraged to use the index of an atlas to find further countries or cities themselves, for other children to arrange alphabetically.

'Searching for information' games can be devised using the local *Yellow Pages*. The children could formulate their own questions about information they might require.

Pages 9–13: Understanding abbreviations

These activity sheets will encourage the children to understand the importance of abbreviations.

Answers

Page 9: a.m. '*ante meridiem*' meaning 'before noon'; s.a.e. stamped addressed envelope; a.s.a.p. as soon as possible; m.p.h. miles per hour; etc. 'et cetera' meaning 'and the rest'; p.m. '*post meridiem*' meaning 'after noon'; c/o care of; km kilometre; mpg miles per gallon.
Page 10: OAP old age pensioner; PM Prime Minister; HRH Her/His Royal Highness; USA United States of America; GP General Practitioner; IOU I owe you; DIY do it yourself; VIP very important person; BBC British Broadcasting Corporation.
Page 11: adj. adjective; cap. capital letter; adv. adverb; v. verb; fem. feminine; e.g. '*exempli gratia*' meaning 'for example'; conj. conjunction; pl. plural; masc. masculine.
Page 12: Strath. Strathclyde; Yorks. Yorkshire; Lancs. Lancashire; Lincs. Lincolnshire; Staffs. Staffordshire; Herts. Hertfordshire; W. Glam. West Glamorgan; Wilts. Wiltshire; Hants Hampshire (no full stop as not a true abbreviation); IOW Isle of Wight; Ferm. Fermanagh.
Page 13: St. Street; Ave. Avenue; Sq. Square; Gdns. Gardens; Dr. Drive; Rd. Road; Pl. Place; Cres. Crescent; Ter. Terrace.

Extension activity

The children could make up their own acronyms for clubs and other activities held in school.

Pages 14–17: Using a dictionary to check definitions (Homophones and Homonyms)

These activities introduce children to the complexity of the English language.

Homophones are words that sound the same but are spelled differently. Encourage the children to look at the words and try to see how the spelling can help with the meaning of the words. For example, an 'isle' is an island or small peninsular. The common letters at the beginning of the two words can help to link the correct meaning and, therefore, correct spelling.

Homonyms are words that are spelled the same but have different meanings according to the sentence within which they occur. Children often have difficulty with these words and it is suggested that the words are not introduced together to the children until they have one of the meanings firmly established.

Extension activities

The children could use dictionaries to find further examples of homophones and homonyms.
Make a game by putting words and their meanings on to separate cards and asking the children to find the pairs.

Pages 18–20: Using a dictionary to encourage scanning (Close clues)

These activity sheets will help children to focus on a page within a dictionary, as these words are relatively close to each other. This will encourage the children to skim the page.

Extension activity

Make a sorting game. Mix up words and their meanings written on to separate cards. The children should then sort the words and correct meanings within a time limit. Timing will make the necessary repetition more interesting.

Pages 21–25: Using a dictionary to check for meaning

These activities encourage children to look carefully at the meaning of words within the text. By making a guess initially, the children will need to read for meaning and use contextual clues. This is then checked by using a dictionary.

Extension activity

The children could work with partners, find some suitable text and formulate their own charts for others to use.

Pages 26–28: Using a thesaurus to extend vocabulary

These activities will extend the children's use of adjectives and allow for some improvisations. Discourage the children from merely exchanging the adjectives around. They should be encouraged to think of alternative adjectives. For example; Amazing bargains, Daring rides, Terrific prizes, Mouth-watering refreshments.

Extension activity

Similar posters could be devised for events held in school.

Pages 29–32: Using a thesaurus for alternative words

These activities are to encourage children to use a thesaurus to discourage their overuse of common words. This is a useful extension and reinforcement activity to complement redrafting their stories.

Dictionary exercises

The following are additional activities that can be done either as whole-class or as group tasks using standard primary dictionaries.

Skimming skills

1 Find that word
Name a word. The first child to find the word reads out the definition and scores a point. Set a limit on the number of points required for an overall winner.

2 First/last word
Ask, 'What is the first/last word in (column ?) on page...?' The winner then selects a word and gives instructions for the group to locate it.

3 Initial hunt
Ask the children to see how quickly they can find the first word beginning with a chosen letter, for example 'p', or, alternatively, how quickly can they find the last word beginning with the letter 'g'. This game encourages them to use their alphabet order knowledge as well as skimming.

Scanning skills

4 Ladder words
Name a word; for example, WORD. The letters are written vertically down the left-hand side of the page and then the letters are written in reverse order in the second column; for example:

W D
O R
R O
D W

The children have to complete the words across, scanning in the dictionary for words that start and end as suggested. For example, the above words could read as follows: WooD, OffeR, RadiO, DraW.

5 Three word blank
Look through the dictionary and select three words together on a page. Tell the group the first and third words and asks the children to identify the word between. For example: 1 made, 2 magazine, 3 maggot. When the winner has found the word he or she could gain an extra point by composing a sentence that includes the word.

6 Definition scanning
Select a page from a junior dictionary and then tell the group the meaning of one of the words on the page. The children must scan the page to find the word that matches the definition and then compose a sentence containing that word. For example, the teacher says, 'Page 30. This means to hold tightly to someone or something.' The child identifies the word as 'cling' and then offers a sentence including the word, such as, 'A squirrel clings tightly to the trunk of a tree with its claws.'

Words and their meanings

7 Prefixes
Give the children one of the following prefixes: ante, trans, tele, photo, semi, pre, post, mis, com. Ask them to list as many words containing that prefix as they can find. For example: telegram, telescope, television, telephone and so on. They should write the words and their definitions.

8 Word of the day
Ask a child to look in the dictionary to find a word whose meaning they do not know. The child should write the word on the board and tell the class what the dictionary says the word means. Then the teacher should ask the group how this word could be used in a sentence. For example, 'tether' could be used in 'The goat was tethered to the post.'

If possible, revisit this word during the day. The children could be asked what the word was at the end of the day and praise given to any child who can make up a sentence using the word.

9 Alliterative sentences

The teacher selects a letter of the alphabet and asks the children to work in pairs to compose an alliterative sentence using only that letter. They can use a dictionary to ensure that they select words that make sense; for example, 'Proud people prefer priceless pearls.' A collection of these sentences could be displayed on the wall for all the class to see.

Words and spelling

10 Check the spelling

Select a 'difficult word' and ask the children to listen to the word while it is said. The children each need to say the word quietly to a neighbour and finally try to write the word. Then write the word on to the board and let the children see how well they did. A mark could be given for every correct letter in its correct order and a bonus mark for any child that wrote the word completely correct. For example, the word chosen might be 'rhinoceros'. If the child offered 'rinoseros', he or she would get eight marks. If a child wrote 'rinhsos', then he or she would get five marks. The 'h' is out of order and therefore does not score.

Finally, the children should then look carefully at the word displayed on the board. The teacher then rubs out the word and the group tries to write it. This activity is especially useful as a way of helping the children with 'topic-specific' vocabulary.

National Curriculum: English

The activities in this book support the following requirements of the PoS for KS2 for the National Curriculum for English:

Speaking and Listening
- Pupils should be taught to use an increasingly varied vocabulary. The range of pupils' vocabulary should be extended and enriched through activities that focus on words and their meanings, including:
  - discussion of more imaginative and adventurous choices of words;
  - consideration of groups of words.

Reading
- They should be introduced to a wide range of literature, and have opportunities to read extensively for their own interest and pleasure, and for information;
- Pupils should read and use a wide range of sources of information, including those not specifically designed for children. The range of non-fiction should include IT-based reference materials, newspapers, encyclopaedias, dictionaries and thesauruses;
- Pupils should be taught how to find information in books and computer-based sources by using organisational devices to help them decide which parts of the material to read closely. They should be given opportunities to read for different purposes, adopting appropriate strategies for the task, including skimming to gain an overall impression, scanning to locate information and detailed reading to obtain specific information. Pupils should be taught to:
  - identify the precise information that they wish to know;
  - use dictionaries, glossaries and thesauruses to explain unfamiliar vocabulary;
  - note the meaning and use of newly encountered words;
- They should be encouraged to use their knowledge gained from reading to develop their understanding of the structure, vocabulary and grammar of standard English.

Writing
- Pupils should be given opportunities to write for varied purposes, understanding that writing is essential to thinking and learning;
- They should write in response to a wide range of stimuli;
- In spelling, pupils should be accumulating a bank of words that they can spell correctly, and should be taught to check spellings and meanings of words, using dictionaries where appropriate. When looking up words, pupils should be taught to apply their knowledge of initial and subsequent letters and the organisation of dictionaries, including headings, abbreviations and other conventions. They should be taught:
  - alternative ways of writing the same sound;
- Pupils should be taught to distinguish between words of similar meaning, to explain the meanings of words and to experiment with choices of vocabulary. Their interest in words should be extended by the discussion of language use and choices.

See inside back cover for Scottish 5-14 Curriculum and Northern Ireland Curriculum links

● Name _____

Countries

These are all countries of the world.
● Put them in alphabetical order.

Argentina
       Albania
  Angola
     America
Austria
      Afghanistan
  Australia
     Algeria

1 _____
2 _____
3 _____
4 _____
5 _____
6 _____
7 _____
8 _____

● Now put these countries into alphabetical order.

1 _____
2 _____
3 _____
4 _____
5 _____
6 _____
7 _____
8 _____

      Belize
  Belgium
      Bangladesh
  Botswana
      Brunei
  Bolivia
      Brazil
  Bulgaria

● ESSENTIALS FOR ENGLISH: Dictionary skills

Name _____

Capital cities

Below are the names of some capital cities.
- Put them in alphabetical order.
- Find out in which country they belong.

City

Country

Tokyo

Delhi

London

Moscow

Brasilia

Prague

Washington D.C.

Tegucigalpa

Beijing

Rome

Buenos Aires

Canberra

Cairo

Paris

Berlin

Madrid

Reykjavik

Dacca

ESSENTIALS FOR ENGLISH: Dictionary skills

● Name _____

Class register

● Put the names opposite into this class register in alphabetical order. The first one has been done for you.

	23rd Oct	30th Oct
Baker, Ann		

Fiona Draper

Simon Drew

Rose West

James Radford

Shahida Prasad

Kay Webb

Sam Rahman

Barbara Raymond

James Drummond

Peter Preston

Martin Barker

Diana Wells

Sue Baldwin

Andrew Price

● ESSENTIALS FOR ENGLISH: Dictionary skills

● Name _____

Advertisers

BARRY'S TOP SHOP *specialising in trainers*
081 594371

BRACKEN
Golf Suppliers. All leading makes
081 637482

W. Bird.
081 538419
Specialist ski shop
Clothing hire
Friendly and helpful service

Football Gear
BOLDENS
The Club Specialist Extensive selection
081 795900

BEARDS
Sports shop
081 696743
ALL THE GEAR

BLADES
Sweater shop
All shapes, sizes and colours.
081 695976

Weight Training Equipment
M.E. Booster
Professional fitness
081 101760

● Put these advertisers in alphabetical order.

Name of firm	Phone number

● ESSENTIALS FOR ENGLISH: Dictionary skills

● Name _____

Abbreviations

● Find out what these abbreviations mean.

a.m.

_____

s.a.e.

_____

a.s.a.p.

_____

m.p.h.

_____

etc.

_____

p.m.

_____

c/o

_____

km

_____

mpg

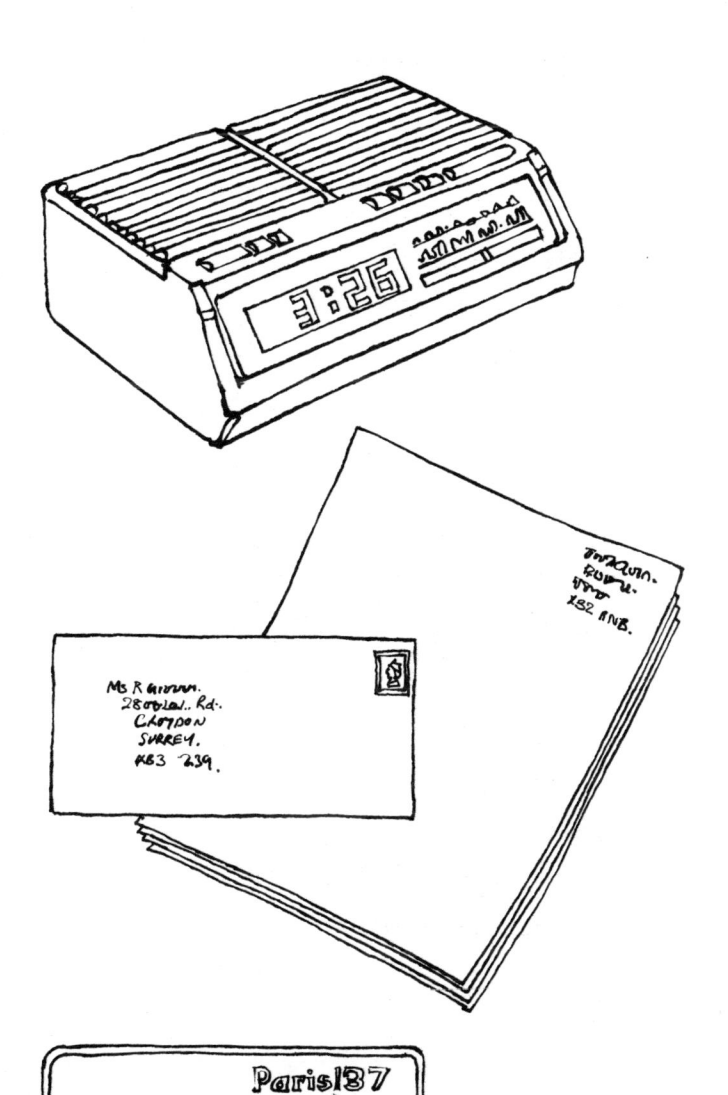

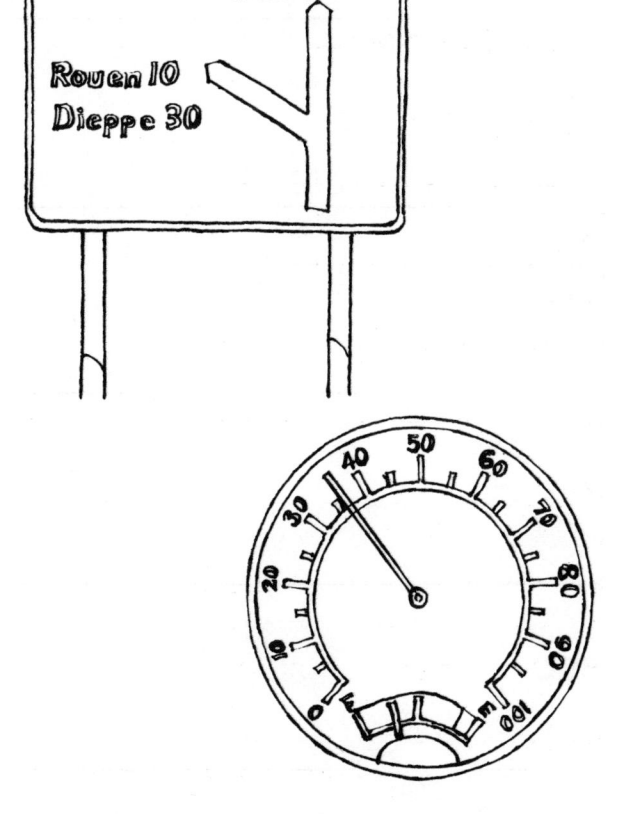

_____

● Name _____

Acronyms

● Find out what these acronyms mean.

OAP

_____

PM

_____

HRH

_____

USA

_____

GP

_____

IOU

_____

DIY

_____

VIP

_____

BBC

_____

● Name _____

Dictionary conventions

These abbreviations are used in dictionaries.
● Find out what they mean.

adj.
_____

cap.
_____

adv.
_____

v.
_____

fem.
_____

e.g.
_____

conj.
_____

pl.
_____

masc.
_____

● ESSENTIALS FOR ENGLISH: Dictionary skills

● Name _____

Counties

The names of many counties have abbreviations. Some of them are marked on the map opposite.
● Find out the full names of these counties and write them on the lines below.

Strath.
_____

Ferm.
_____

Yorks.
_____

Lancs.
_____

Lincs.
_____

Staffs.
_____

W. Glam.
_____

Herts.
_____

Hants
_____

Wilts.
_____

IOW
_____

● Which county do you live in? _____

● ESSENTIALS FOR ENGLISH: Dictionary skills

● Name _____

Addresses

These abbreviations are used in letters and addresses.
● Write each word out in full under its abbreviation.

St.
_____
Ave.

_____
Sq.
_____
Gdns.

_____

Dr.
_____
Rd.

_____
Ter.
Pl.
_____
_____
Cres.

_____

● ESSENTIALS FOR ENGLISH: Dictionary skills

Name _____

Homophones – 1

These words are called homophones. They are words that sound the same but are spelled differently. They have different meanings too.

● Find the meaning of the other word in each pair in a dictionary. The first one has been done for you.

---

aisle – a path between seats, usually in a church, bus or cinema.

isle – an island or small peninsula.

---

alter – to change.

altar – _____

---

bare – empty or without any covering.

bear – _____

---

horse – an animal with hooves, used for riding.

hoarse – _____

---

pain – a feeling you have when you are hurt.

pane – _____

---

coarse – rough, not smooth.

course – _____

● ESSENTIALS FOR ENGLISH: Dictionary skills

Name _____

Homophones – 2

These words are called homophones. They are words that sound the same but are spelled differently. They have different meanings too.

● Find out the meaning of the second word in each pair below.

way   – a road or path.

weigh – _____

boar   – a wild pig.

bore   – _____

manner – the way something is done.

manor – _____

dough – a mixture of flour and water.

doe   – _____

reign – to be king or queen.

rain   – _____

herd   – cattle that feed together.

heard – _____

● ESSENTIALS FOR ENGLISH: Dictionary skills

● Name _____

Homonyms – 1

Homonyms are words with the same spellings, but different meanings.

● Find two meanings for these words.
The first one has been done for you.

> well – in good health.
>
> well – a shaft sunk into the ground to obtain water or oil.

> funnel – _____
>
> funnel – _____

> staff – _____
>
> staff – _____

> dart – _____
>
> dart – _____

> rest – _____
>
> rest – _____

> stamp – _____
>
> stamp – _____

● ESSENTIALS FOR ENGLISH: Dictionary skills

● Name _____

Homonyms – 2

Homonyms are words with the same spellings, but different meanings.

● Find two meanings for these words.

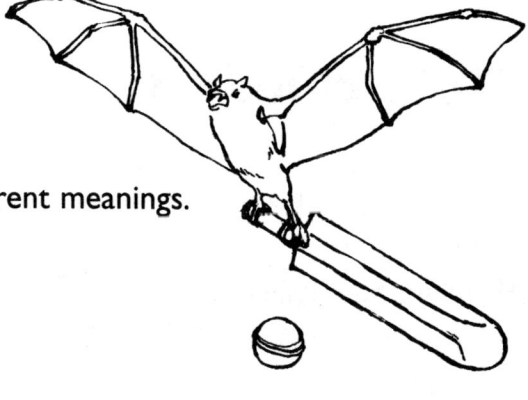

bat – _____
bat – _____

set – _____
set – _____

patient – _____
patient – _____

yield – _____
yield – _____

stalk – _____
stalk – _____

band – _____
band – _____

ESSENTIALS FOR ENGLISH: Dictionary skills

● Name _____

Close clues – 1

These clues are for pairs of words which are close to each other in the dictionary.

● Fill in the missing words. The clues will help you to find them.

Clue	Answer
A fast aeroplane.	j _____
A woolly sweater.	j _____
A place where children go to learn.	s _____
A tool with two blades for cutting.	s _____
A machine people watch.	t _____
The bad mood someone is in.	t _____
Hair growing on a man's chin.	b _____
Any big animal.	b _____
A story that teaches people something.	f _____
A building where things are made by machine.	f _____

● Make up a similar pair of clues yourself and try them on a friend.

● ESSENTIALS FOR ENGLISH: Dictionary skills

● Name _____

Close clues – 2

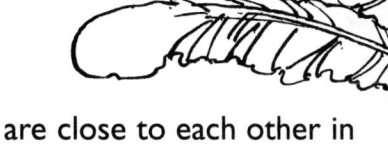

These clues are for pairs of words which are close to each other in the dictionary.

● Fill in the missing words. The clues will help you to find them.

| A large feather. | pl _____ |
| More than one. | pl _____ |

| To struggle with someone. | wr _____ |
| Old people usually have them. | wr _____ |

| A set of three things or people. | tr _____ |
| Very pleased, successful. | tr _____ |

| Words that say something important. | st _____ |
| A stone or metal model of a person. | st _____ |

| How good or bad something is. | qu _____ |
| An amount. | qu _____ |

● Make up a similar pair of clues yourself and try them on a friend.

● ESSENTIALS FOR ENGLISH: Dictionary skills

● Name _____

Close clues – 3

These words are close to each other in the dictionary.
● Write a clue to each word.

| design | |
| desire | |

| exact | |
| examine | |

| permission | |
| persist | |

| implore | |
| impress | |

| transform | |
| transparent | |

● Choose two words yourself and let a friend try to write the clues.

● ESSENTIALS FOR ENGLISH: Dictionary skills

● Name _____

The frog prince

● Read this story.

> The king had several comely daughters. His youngest daughter was the most beautiful and was admired by everyone. The king gave her a golden ball to play with, which she treasured above all her other toys.
>
> One day, while she was playing with the ball, she threw it into the air and it fell, with a splash, into an ancient well. The princess was very upset and sobbed bitterly. She had lost her most precious possession. She did not notice a large, repulsive frog who had leaped from the well and sat next to her.

● Find the words below in the story and underline them; guess the meaning of each word and then check their meanings.

	Guess	Meaning
comely		
admired		
treasured		
ancient		
precious		
repulsive		

● ESSENTIALS FOR ENGLISH: Dictionary skills   21

● Name _____

The fox

● Read the following information.

Foxes are found all over Britain. They live in woods and copses, but often visit towns to scavenge in dustbins for their food. They catch rats and mice as well.

Foxes are slender creatures with bushy tails called brushes. The brush is tipped with white. Foxes have an acute sense of smell and this makes them difficult to approach. If a fox is hunted, he can climb trees, double back on his tracks, go into water or mingle with sheep. This could be the reason why this animal is called, 'cunning or wily old fox!'

● Find the words below in the information and underline them; guess the meaning of each word and then check their meanings.

	Guess	Meaning
slender		
copse		
scavenge		
acute		
mingle		
wily		

● ESSENTIALS FOR ENGLISH: Dictionary skills

● Name _____

The grey squirrel

● Read the following information.

There are two species of squirrel, the red squirrel and the grey squirrel. Both are rodents. The grey squirrel was introduced into Great Britain from America in the nineteenth century.

Both species of squirrel are active climbers with long bushy tails. They sit upright to nibble at nuts, seeds, buds, berries and fungi. When they have surplus food they bury it for a future time. Grey squirrels harm trees by gnawing at the main stem to get at the sweet sappy layers beneath the bark.

Grey squirrels will live in suburban parks and gardens and become tame enough to feed from the hand.

● Find the words below in the information and underline them; guess the meaning of each word and then check their meanings.

	Guess	Meaning
active		
species		
surplus		
harm		
sappy		
suburban		

● ESSENTIALS FOR ENGLISH: Dictionary skills

● Name _____

The badger

● Read the following information.

The badger is a mammal that is found in all parts of the British Isles. It is a nocturnal creature and it lives underground in a sett. The sett is usually situated in a woodland hillside. There are chambers and tunnels in the home and more than one entrance.

Badgers eat a variety of food including worms, mice, voles, frogs, snails and wasps. They also eat grass, blackberries and windfall apples.

The most distinctive feature of the badger is its white head with a black stripe over each ear and eye.

It has no enemies except man.

● Find the words below in the information and underline them; guess the meaning of each word and then check their meanings.

	Guess	Meaning
mammal		
nocturnal		
variety		
enemies		
situated		
distinctive		

● ESSENTIALS FOR ENGLISH: Dictionary skills

Name _____

The rabbit

● Read the following information.

> Rabbits were introduced into this country from France in the twelfth century and were highly valued for their meat. They are social animals and live in colonies or warrens. The warrens connect with tunnels, runs and emergency exits. The rabbits come out to feed at dawn and at dusk. They eat any fresh green food that is available. They nibble at the bark of trees and eat the shoots and also eat cereals, root crops and grass. They have become one of the most destructive agricultural pests.

● Find the words below in the information and underline them; guess the meaning of each word and then check their meanings.

	Guess	Meaning
introduced		
colonies		
emergency		
available		
destructive		
cereals		

● ESSENTIALS FOR ENGLISH: Dictionary skills

Name _____

Adjectives – 1

● Use a thesaurus to help you to replace the adjectives marked in bold in the poster below.

School Fair

Fantastic bargains

Exhilarating rides

Brilliant side-shows

Delicious refreshments

Exciting prizes

School Fair

_____ bargains

_____ rides

_____ side-shows

_____ refreshments

_____ prizes

● ESSENTIALS FOR ENGLISH: Dictionary skills

Name _____

Adjectives – 2

ICE-CREAM TASTING FREE!!

Come and try these delicious flavours:

rich and smooth chocolate;

wholesome and scrumptious walnut;

super and sweet strawberry;

luscious and tasty mango.

● Use a thesaurus to help you find different words to describe the flavours of ice-cream.

ICE-CREAM TASTING FREE!!

Come and try these _____ flavours:

_____ and _____ chocolate;

_____ and _____ walnut;

_____ and _____ strawberry;

_____ and _____ mango.

● ESSENTIALS FOR ENGLISH: Dictionary skills

Find another word

● Use a thesaurus to help you to replace the words marked in bold in the advertisement below.

A CHILDREN'S MAGAZINE

Funny cartoons

Video **summaries**

BUY ONE and TRY ONE Today

Book **information**

Exciting computer games

New and **different**

A CHILDREN'S MAGAZINE

_____ cartoons

Video _____

BUY ONE and TRY ONE Today

Book _____

_____ computer games

New and _____

ESSENTIALS FOR ENGLISH: Dictionary skills

Name _____

Replacing 'nice'

Nice isn't the only word that would fit in these spaces.
- Read the passage through first.
- Now think of some alternative words.

Dear Uncle Stan,

Thank you very much for my birthday money, it was _____ (nice)

of you. I spent the money you sent me at the 'Rainbow Theme Park'.

It was _____ (nice) and I had a _____ (nice)

time. I went on the 'Water Splash', that was really _____ (nice),

although I did get rather wet! My favourite ride was the 'Roller-coaster'. It was

very _____ (nice) , it frightened me a lot. The track was

_____ (nice) and steep and I was turned upside down twice.

Fortunately, I was strapped in. I had a _____ (nice) lunch before

I went on the ghost train. That was really _____ (nice) as well.

Thanks again for the _____ (nice) present.

Love from,

Sam.

ESSENTIALS FOR ENGLISH: Dictionary skills

29

● Name _____

Replacing 'said'

Said isn't the only word that would fit in these spaces.
● Read the passage through first.
● Now think of some alternative words.

The Professor was experimenting again!

'Oh, my goodness,' he _____ (said) , 'I think I've done it.

'Martin,' he _____ (said) , 'Come quickly, I think I've done it!'

Martin rushed in. 'What?' he _____ (said) .'What have you done?'

'Look at me,' _____ (said) the Professor. 'Can't you see?'

'No,' _____ (said) Martin.

'Look again,' _____ (said) the Professor.

'Oh, my goodness,' _____ (said) Martin, 'you are growing smaller.

'Quick,' _____ (said) the Professor. 'Put me on the table.'

'Why?' _____ (said) Martin.

'So you can still see me,' _____ (said) the Professor, as he reached the size of an apple.

● ESSENTIALS FOR ENGLISH: Dictionary skills

● Name _____

Replacing 'very'

Very isn't the only word that would fit in these spaces.

● Read the passage through first.
● Now think of some alternative words.

Jane was walking _____ fast along the cliff path. She
                      very

was _____ careful as the path was _____
         very   very

steep and uneven.

'Help! Help!'

Jane heard a shout. She looked round feeling _____
                                                    very

puzzled. 'Where are you?' she shouted.

'Over here,' said a _____ frightened voice. 'Look down!'
                         very

Jane looked down and saw the _____ white face of a
                                    very

_____ small girl clinging to a tree overhanging the path edge.
     very

'Oh, my goodness,' said Jane, 'what shall I do? Shall I go for help?'

'There isn't time,' said the girl, 'I feel _____ unsafe and
                                               very

I'm losing my grip.'

'Be _____ careful,' said Jane. 'I'll try and pull you up.'
         very

She pulled and pulled, _____ hard.
                             very

'Thank you,' said the girl, 'I think you saved my life.' Jane grinned, she

was _____ relieved.
         very

'Think nothing of it,' she said, 'it's just as well I came along.'

● ESSENTIALS FOR ENGLISH: Dictionary skills   31

● Name _____

Replacing various words

● Use a thesaurus to find some **alternative** words to write into these spaces. Read the passage through first.

A young shepherd was sitting on a hillside _____ (eating)

his lunch and feeling very _____ (lonely). Suddenly a

_____ (large) bird flew down in front of him. The

shepherd felt _____ (afraid). He wondered what the

bird intended to do. Was the bird going to attack him or attack

the lambs grazing nearby?

_____ (Shaking) with fear he threw some bread to the

bird. The bird _____ (jumped) forward, took the bread

and, much to the shepherd's relief, flew off.

He came every day after that and shared the young shepherd's

lunch. Soon he _____ (took) the bread

from the shepherd's hand. He was not an enemy, he was a

friend. The young shepherd was _____ (lonely)

no longer.

● ESSENTIALS FOR ENGLISH: Dictionary skills   32